Contents

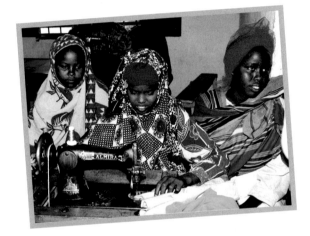

Discovering Somalia

Somalia became an independent country in 1960. Since then, it has faced many difficulties, including ineffective government, civil war and famine. Today, Somalia is one of the poorest countries in the world and life is difficult for the Somali people.

Colonization and independence

Because of its position between sub-Saharan Africa and the countries of Arabia and south-west Asia, the region that is now Somalia was an important trade route for many years. Somali nomads began to move into the area in around the tenth century. Europeans began exploring this part of Africa in the 1800s and by the start of the next century, Britain and Italy had both colonized parts of Somalia. In 1960, Somalia gained independence when British Somaliland and Italian Somaliland were united.

This map shows the different regions of Somalia and its border countries.

A country divided

The people of Somalia are divided into hundreds of different groups, called clans. After independence, these clans began fighting each other. Although Somalia started out as a democracy, in 1969 the military took control. General Mohamed Siad Barre ruled Somalia until 1991, when he was overthrown. As the clans of different regions claimed independence and fought each other for control of land, Somalia descended into civil war.

DID YOU KNOW?
The five points of the star on the Somali flag represent the five historical regions in which Somali people settled: British and Italian Somaliland, Djibouti, Ogaden and the Northern Frontier District.

discover countries

Somalia

RC

This b

The l
a furt

Sonya Newland

WAYLAND

Published in paperback in 2014
Copyright Wayland 2014

Wayland
Hachette Children's Books
338 Euston Road
London NW1 3BH

Wayland Australia
Level 17/207 Kent Street,
Sydney, NSW 2000

Concept design: Jason Billin
Editor: Sonya Newland
Design: 320 Design Ltd
Proofreader: Alice Harman

Produced for Wayland by
White-Thomson Publishing Ltd

www.wtpub.co.uk
+44 (0)843 2087 460

British Library Cataloguing in Publication Data

Newland, Sonya.
Somalia. -- (Discover countries)
1. Somalia -- Juvenile literature.
I. Title II. Series
967.7'3053-dc23

ISBN-13: 978 0 7502 8088 4
Printed in China

2 4 6 8 10 9 7 5 3 1

Wayland is a division of Hachette Children's Books
an Hachette UK company
www.hachette.co.uk

All data in this book was researched in 2011
and has been collected from the latest sources available at that time.

Picture credits

1, UN Photo/Milton Grant; 3 (top), UN Photo/Milton Grant; 3 (bottom), CharlesFred/Creative Commons License; 4 (map), Stefan Chabluk;
5, Getty Images; 6, Corbis/Ed Harris/Reuters; 7, Fotolia/Abdelhamid Kalai; 8, Frank Keillor/Creative Commons License; 9, UN Photo/Stuart Price;
10, UN Photo/Stuart Price; 11, Dreamstime/Sadic Gulek; 12, Photolibrary/Robert Harding; 13, Travel Library/Eye Ubiquitous; 14, Getty Images/AFP;
15, Getty Images/AFP; 16, Photolibrary/Eye Ubiquitous; 17, Corbis/Ismail Warsameh/Xinhua Press; 18, Getty Images/MCT; 19, UN Photo/Milton
Grant; 20, Getty Images/AFP; 21, Getty Images/MCT; 22, Corbis/Shabele Media/X02084/Reuters; 23, Travel Library/Eye Ubiquitous;
24, CharlesFred/Creative Commons License; 25, Wikipedia/Maxamad; 26, Travel Library/Eye Ubiquitous; 27, UN Photo/Milton Grant; 28, Fotolia/
Abdelhamid Kalai; 29, Shutterstock/Anke van Wyk
Cover images, Travel Library/Eye Ubiquitous (left), Getty Images/De Agostini (right)

In 1991, the northern part of the country declared its independence as the Republic of Somaliland. In 1998, an area in the north-east was established as an autonomous region called Puntland. There is no permanent central government in Somalia. Instead there is a transitional federal government, which only controls a few small parts of Somalia.

Drought and famine

In 2011, lack of rain caused drought to spread through parts of East Africa, including Somalia. Crops would not grow and there were severe food shortages. As the famine worsened, thousands of Somalis left the country and settled in refugee camps in Kenya and Ethiopia. Since 1991, more than a million people have died as a result of the civil war, famine and disease in Somalia.

◆ Somalis line up to receive food from an aid agency in Mogadishu. These people have fled the famine in southern Somalia.

Somalia statistics

Area: 637,657 sq km (246,201 sq miles)

Capital city: Mogadishu

Government type: No permanent national government; transitional federal government

Bordering countries: Djibouti, Ethiopia, Kenya

Currency: Somali shilling

Language: Somali (official), Arabic, Italian, English

Landscape and climate

Somalia is warm all year round, but unlike many other countries around the Equator, Somalia does not have a true tropical climate with regular rainfall. Some of the highest temperatures in the world have been recorded in Somalia, and droughts are common.

Four seasons

Somalia's climate is divided into four seasons – two rainy and two dry. The main rainy season (*gu*) lasts from April to June, and the second (*dayr*) lasts from October to December. The two dry seasons (*jilaal* and *xagaa*) fall in between. Average rainfall across the country is low – only 500 mm (20 inches) a year.

Facts at a glance

Land area: 637,660 sq km (242,216 sq miles)

Water area: 10,320 sq km (3,985 sq miles)

Highest point: Shimbiris 2,416 m (7,927 ft)

Lowest point: Indian Ocean 0 m (0 ft)

Longest river: Shabeelle River 1,820 km (1,130 miles)

Coastline: 3,025 km (1,880 miles)

▼ During the long dry seasons, most rivers in Somalia dry up completely, leaving dry riverbeds known as wadis.

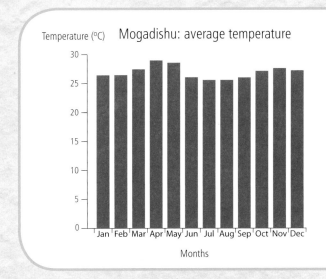

Temperature (°C) **Mogadishu: average temperature**

Months

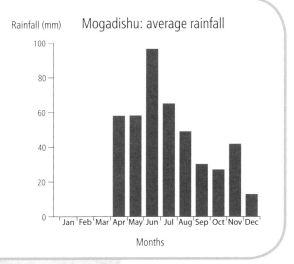

Rainfall (mm) **Mogadishu: average rainfall**

Months

Plains, plateaus and highlands

Most of Somalia is made up of flat, semi-desert plains and plateaus. These areas are mainly dry scrubland with just a few trees. In the north, parallel to the Gulf of Aden coast, is a plain called the Guban. South of the Guban is Somalia's only highland region, the Karkaar Mountains. Here stands Somalia's highest point – the mountain Shimbiris. A large central plain stretches southwards from the mountains and then westwards into the Ogaden Desert in Ethiopia. Dust storms often sweep across the plains during the dry season.

Rivers of the south

Two main rivers flow through Somalia. The Jubba River begins on the border with Ethiopia and flows southwards into the Indian Ocean. The Shabeelle River flows south-eastwards from its source in Ethiopia into Somalia and towards the capital, Mogadishu. In the rainy season the Shabeelle sometimes joins up with the Jubba in the far south of the country, but it often dries up before reaching the Jubba. The land between the two rivers is the most fertile in Somalia. Elsewhere, vegetation is sparse and there is little shade from the burning sun.

△ Typically, there is no rainfall in Mogadishu between January and March.

DID YOU KNOW?

The Jubba River runs for 875 km (545 miles) through Somalia. It the only river in the country that flows all year round.

▽ Somalia has the longest coastline in Africa, stretching uninterrupted for 3,025 km (1,880 miles) from the Gulf of Aden and then southwards along the Indian Ocean.

Population and health

The population of Somalia is believed to be nearly 10 million. However, it is difficult to make an accurate population count. This is partly because many Somalis lead a nomadic lifestyle, but also because thousands of people have moved around or even left the country altogether because of the civil war.

Ethnic make-up

More than 85 per cent of the population are Somalis. Nearly all the rest belong to an ethnic African group called the Bantu. There are also around 30,000 Arabs living in Somalia, as well as a small Italian population. Some Somalis settled in the Ogaden region of Ethiopia and in northern Kenya many years ago, but thousands more have moved to these countries in recent years in search of food and a better life.

The clans

Ethnic Somalis belong to groups called clans. Each clan claims to trace its ancestry back to a single father. Clans include the Sab people who live between the Jubba and Shabeelle rivers, the Daarood clan of north-eastern Somalia and the Ogaden region, the Hawiye of southern and central areas, and the Isaaq in the north and north-west. There is a great deal of conflict between different clans, as they fight for land and resources.

Facts at a glance

Total population: 9.9 million
Life expectancy at birth: 50.4 years
Children dying before the age of five: 18%
Ethnic composition: Somali 85%, Bantu and other non-Somali 15% (including 30,000 Arabs)

▼ The Somali people all share the same language, religion and cultural traditions, but they are divided by their membership of different clans.

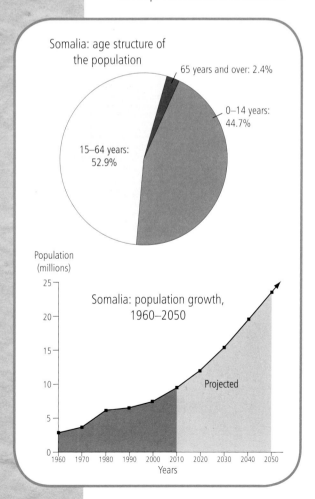

▲ Women watch over their malnourished children in a hospital in Mogadishu. International organizations are working in hospitals in the cities to help victims of the famine.

Disease and health

Somalia has one of the highest birth rates in the world. However, many young children – about 106 for every 1,000 babies born – die before the age of one because they do not receive basic health care. For every 100,000 people there are only 0.5 doctors and two nurses. Food prices are so high that most people cannot afford to buy enough to eat, and they become ill through malnourishment. Polluted water supplies also spread disease among the Somali people.

DID YOU KNOW?
Nearly half of the Somali population is under 14 years old. Only 2.4 per cent of Somalis are over the age of 65.

Somalia: age structure of the population

65 years and over: 2.4%

0–14 years: 44.7%

15–64 years: 52.9%

Population (millions)

Somalia: population growth, 1960–2050

Projected

Years

Settlements and living

The majority of the people in Somalia live a nomadic lifestyle based on farming and raising livestock. A few farmers have made permanent settlements, mainly in the south of the country. Less than one-third of the population lives in towns and cities.

Life in the cities

The main city in Somalia is the capital, Mogadishu. Other big cities include the ports of Kismayo and Merca in the south and Berbera in the north.

Buildings in the cities are often constructed in the Arabic style, made of whitewashed brick that reflects the sun and keeps the inside cool. Even in the cities, many homes do not have electricity or running water. Slums have grown up on the outskirts of Somalia's towns and cities, as people move there to escape the harsh life in rural areas.

Nomads

Somali nomads move around the country to find the best grazing land for their livestock. They build temporary camps from dome-shaped tents called *aqals*. These are made from pole frames covered in animal hides or woven mats, which are easily taken down when it is time for the group to move on.

> **Facts at a glance**
>
> **Urban population:** 37.76% (3.6 million)
>
> **Rural population:** 62.24% (5.9 million)
>
> **Population of largest city:** 2 million (Mogadishu)

▼ Mogadishu was once a thriving port city on the Indian Ocean, but many homes, shops and other buildings have been destroyed in the civil war.

Inside the *aqal* is usually just a bed, and daily activities such as washing and cooking are done outside. The nomads do not have many belongings, and they only carry essential items such as cooking utensils with them.

Farming settlements

Farmers in permanent settlements live in dwellings rather like the *aqal* of the nomads. Their round huts are called *mundals*, and have a pole frame covered in mud with a thatched roof. These settlements are mostly found in the region between the Jubba and Shabeelle rivers, where the land is most fertile.

⚫ More than 400,000 Somalis now live in the Dadaab refugee camp, just over the Somali border in Kenya. This is the largest refugee complex in the world.

DID YOU KNOW?
Nearly 1.5 million Somalis have been displaced by the civil war. Many of them now live in refugee camps either in Somalia or in Kenya or Ethiopia.

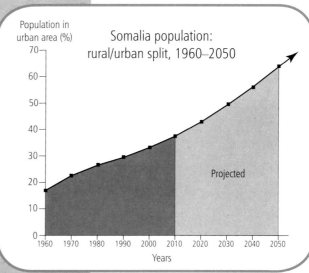

Population in urban area (%)

Somalia population: rural/urban split, 1960–2050

Projected

Years

Family life

The family and the clan are very important to Somalis, and are at the heart of Somali customs and daily life. In nomadic communities, several sub-clans will often live together, and members of these groups may marry each other.

Family roles

In nomadic communities men will take care of the camels or cattle, which are the most valuable livestock. Younger boys and girls may look after the sheep and goats. Women are responsible for looking after the camp and raising the children. In urban areas, life for both men and women is more westernized, and women may go out to work rather than staying at home.

Facts at a glance

Average children per childbearing woman:
6.35 children

Average household size:
5.8 people

▽ Men in rural areas may spend periods of time away from their family, driving herds of camels and other livestock to suitable grazing land.

Marriage customs

As Sunni Muslims, Somali men can have up to four wives – as long as they have enough money to look after them and any children they have. In the cities, the different wives and their families usually live in different houses. In rural areas, a man may live in a single household with all his wives and children.

In rural areas, senior members of a family or clan often arrange marriages for younger members. The groom pays a 'bride price' of money or livestock to his bride's family. If a woman marries a man from another clan, she then becomes a member of her husband's clan.

Extended families

Large families with seven or eight children born to a single wife are quite common in Somalia. It is also usual for extended families to live together, with older members staying with their children and grandchildren. Family bonds are strong, and if young people move to the cities for work or education they are likely to stay with family members who live there.

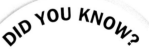 Somalis place great importance on children. The more children a woman has, the more important she is considered to be within the family.

DID YOU KNOW?

Divorce is usually initiated by the man in Somalia. A man can divorce his wife by saying 'I divorce you' three times to her.

Religion and beliefs

Almost everyone in Somalia is a Sunni Muslim – a branch of Islam – and in fact it is forbidden to promote any other religion. Despite this, there is a tiny group of Christians in the country, made up of Bantu peoples who converted to Christianity during the colonial period.

Beliefs and practices

The rituals and beliefs of Islam are an essential part of everyday life in Somalia. Mosques – Muslim places of worship – can be found in every town and city. Even in remote areas, nomadic peoples may set up a special area for prayer in their camps.

A respected man in the group is appointed as a religious leader called a *wadad*. He is responsible for leading the people in prayer five times a day and presiding over religious rites and festivals. Like other Muslims, Somalis also believe in spirits called *jinn*, which can bring people good or bad luck.

DID YOU KNOW? The Yibir people are a small Somali clan who travel the country performing special rituals. They are often called on to bless newborn children or newly married couples, in return for which they are given gifts.

▶ Crowds gather for prayer at the Isbaheysiga Mosque in Mogadishu. This mosque can accommodate 10,000 people and is the largest in the Horn of Africa.

Festivals and celebrations

Somalis celebrate the same religious holidays as Muslims all over the world. The holiest time in the Islamic calendar is the month of fasting called Ramadan, when Muslims do not eat or drink between dawn and dusk. At the end of Ramadan, there is a festival called Eid ul-Fitr. This lasts for three days, during which people pray and exchange gifts. They may kill a goat or sheep to provide a feast for family and friends.

Sufism in Somalia

Sufism is an ancient and mystical form of Islam. There are many followers of Sufism in Somalia, and they have established their own farming communities in the south of the country. Sufis, or 'dervishes', are famous for their whirling dance, which allows them to go into a trance to achieve inner peace.

⬛ During the festival of Eid ul-Fitr, street markets sell small gifts for people to give to their friends as part of the celebrations that mark the end of Ramadan.

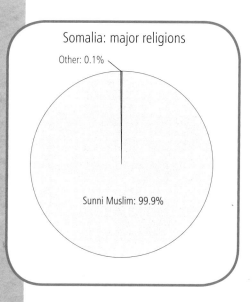

Somalia: major religions

Other: 0.1%

Sunni Muslim: 99.9%

Education and learning

Since the civil war began, there has been no effective education system in Somalia, and many schools have been destroyed in the fighting. As a result, few Somali children have the opportunity to attend school and literacy rates are among the lowest in the world.

City schooling

Most schools are in the towns and cities, and are paid for by donations made by parents or other members of the community. Some schools charge a fee for attending. This means that only wealthy parents can afford to educate their children. The availability and standards of schooling are better in the independent regions of Somaliland and Puntland. These have their own government departments to manage the education system.

In primary schools, children are taught in their own language – Somali. They learn many of the same subjects as children do elsewhere in the world, including maths, geography, history and PE, as well as Arabic and Islamic studies. If children go on to secondary school, they are taught in English. There are also Qur'anic schools in Somalia, where children receive religious instruction.

▼ Children take part in an activity during morning assembly at a primary school in the city of Baidoa.

Rural schooling

Children who live in rural areas are even less likely to receive a proper education than those in towns. In nomadic and farming settlements, children are needed to help their families run the farm or to look after livestock, so there is little time for school. However, some rural communities have schools that children attend when they can.

Higher education

Before the 1990s, there was only one national university in Somalia. Since then, many more universities and colleges have been built, including Mogadishu University, which was named as one of the top 30 universities in Africa in 2011. However, only those who can pay are able to study for a university degree. Efforts are being made to encourage children to go on to higher education. Sometimes young people are given scholarships to help them go to university.

▼ These female students are studying at university in Mogadishu. Despite the civil war, more and more colleges and universities are being built throughout Somalia, Somaliland and Puntland.

Employment and economy

Around 60 per cent of Somalis live in poverty. This means they live on less than US$1 a day, making Somalia one of the poorest countries in the world. Despite civil war, drought and famine, however, Somalia's economy is still growing at around 2.6 per cent a year.

Jobs in the country and city

More than half of Somalis work as herders or farmers in remote rural regions. It is hard for these people to make enough money to survive. Most of the land is too dry to grow crops, and finding food and water for animals is difficult. The recent drought has made this worse.

Facts at a glance

Contributions to GDP:
  agriculture: 60.2%
  industry: 7.4%
  services: 32.4%
Labour force:
  agriculture: 71%
  industry and services: 29%
Female labour force:
  41% of total
Unemployment rate: No data available

🔻 Building work in cities like Mogadishu and Bossaso attracts many Somalis, but also draws workers from neighbouring countries such as Ethiopia.

In the towns and cities, people work in factories that process food products. Other jobs include work as blacksmiths, craftsmen or as teachers at colleges and universities. There is also a great deal of building work going on in Somalia's cities, which provides jobs for construction workers.

Women at work

Traditionally, women in Somalia did not have jobs outside the home. However, as many men have died in the civil war or of disease, more women have had to find work to support themselves. Some international organizations have established programmes to help women set up their own businesses, such as running street stalls or shops. In the cities, women may also work in shops or offices.

An informal economy

Many people in Somalia work in what is called the informal sector. This is when no records are kept of someone's work and so no tax is paid on the money they earn. It is easy to work in the informal sector in Somalia because there is no effective government.

The Somali economy is helped by remittances – money sent back to Somalia by Somalis who have settled in other countries. Remittances are thought to be as much as US$1.6 billion a year.

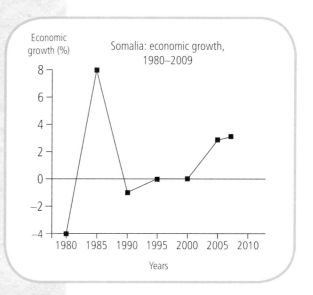

Economic growth (%)

Somalia: economic growth, 1980–2009

Years

DID YOU KNOW?
Somali pirates are groups of Somalis who attack foreign ships in the Indian Ocean or the Gulf of Aden, and then hold the cargo and crew hostage until a ransom is paid.

▶ *These young girls are learning how to sew as part of a programme to teach women skills to help them find a job.*

Industry and trade

The main industries in Somalia are livestock and agriculture. Together, these make up just over 60 per cent of GDP (the total value of goods and services in one year). Trade and industry in Somalia are badly affected because transport systems are so poor, which means that it is difficult to move goods around the country.

Exports and imports

Somalia's main trading partners are countries on the Arabian Peninsula, especially the United Arab Emirates, Yemen and Oman. Somaliland trades with Ethiopia, too. Sheep, goats and cattle are the main exports, along with bananas, fish and animal hides.

▼ Dock workers unload food from a ship in the port of Mogadishu.

Because Somalia does not have many accessible resources or a strong manufacturing industry, it has to import many goods from other countries. Major imports include transportation equipment, machinery and building materials such as cement and iron. The cost of Somalia's imports is nearly twice what the country makes from exports.

Manufacturing

Many industries were shut down in the early years of the civil war. Today, Somalia only has a small manufacturing industry. This is mainly based around the processing of agricultural products. Factories in Somalia's cities process meat and fish. There are also sugar refineries, leather tanneries and textile factories.

Managing money

One industry that has thrived in Somalia is money transfers. Since the 1990s, there has been no official banking sector in the country. To help manage all the remittances that come from Somalis living in other countries, there are money-transfer companies, called *Hawala*. People overseas give their money to a *Hawala*, and an agent pays that amount to the recipient in Somalia. The charges made by the *Hawala* for this service are much less than those made by Western money-transfer companies.

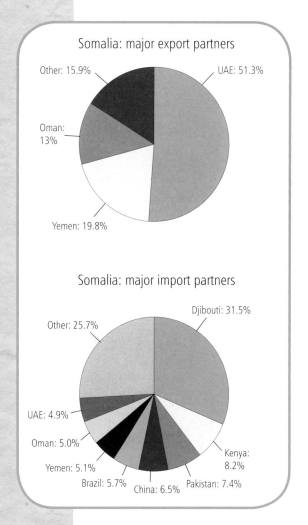

Somalia: major export partners

Other: 15.9%
UAE: 51.3%
Oman: 13%
Yemen: 19.8%

Somalia: major import partners

Other: 25.7%
Djibouti: 31.5%
UAE: 4.9%
Oman: 5.0%
Yemen: 5.1%
Kenya: 8.2%
Brazil: 5.7%
China: 6.5%
Pakistan: 7.4%

▶ Somaliland has its own currency, the Somaliland shilling, which market traders like these will exchange for other currencies.

Farming and food

Farming and raising livestock are the most important activities in Somalia, and about two-thirds of the land is used for grazing livestock such as camels, cattle, sheep and goats. This is the main livelihood of the nomadic Somalis.

Farming and fishing

Most of the land in Somalia is too dry to grow crops. However, in the small areas of fertile land between the Shabeelle and Jubba rivers, farmers cultivate bananas, sugar cane, sorghum, corn and cotton. Despite Somalia's long coastline, there is only a small fishing industry, based mainly in the north. Tuna and shark are caught here. Fish stocks have been depleted by poaching, and the activities of Somali pirates in the Indian Ocean and the Gulf of Aden have also affected the fishing industry.

Facts at a glance

Farmland: 1.6% of total land area

Main agricultural exports: lemons, limes, meat, animal skins, cotton

Main agricultural imports: maize, refined sugar, sorghum, wheat flour, raw sugar

Average daily calorie intake: no data available

▼ In farming settlements, women help tend the crops as well as looking after the children.

Food

The livestock raised by Somali herdsmen provide the main source of meat, but in fact meat is usually only served at feasts or special occasions. Sorghum and rice are the staple food of the nomads, who also drink the milk from camels, goats and cows. In farming communities, people eat boiled millet, rice, vegetables and fruit. They make a corn bread called *muufo*. As Muslims, Somalis do not eat pork or drink alcohol.

In towns and cities, many people enjoy eating out at restaurants. Arabic food is popular, as well as international dishes. In big cities like Mogadishu, restaurants serve Chinese and European dishes.

International aid

Drought, conflict and poverty have resulted in severe famine in parts of Somalia and elsewhere in East Africa. The United Nations (UN) has launched aid programmes to distribute food to the Somali people. However, the civil war makes it dangerous for aid workers, and often the food does not reach the people who need it most.

⬤ At a family meal, men are usually served first, then women and children eat separately later on. It is traditional to take food from the bowl with the right hand.

DID YOU KNOW?

In the cities, Italian food is a favourite among Somalis, a leftover from the Italian colonial era.

Transport and communications

It is not easy to travel around in Somalia because the roads are in such bad condition. This affects the country's economy, because goods cannot be easily transported and people cannot work in different places. There are plans for improving the transport infrastructure, but this will take many years.

Getting around

There are no railways at all in Somalia, and hardly any of the roads are paved, which makes getting around difficult. Journeys can be uncomfortable because the roads are full of potholes. In the rainy seasons, it is almost impossible to reach remote areas. People who live in rural areas tend to stay in their villages, or walk if they need to go somewhere.

🔻 Donkeys and makeshift carts are a common means of transport in Somalia, and can be seen in both rural areas and city streets.

In towns and cities, people get around by bus or truck. Those who need to travel greater distances between Somalia's main centres usually fly. Small private airlines are booming in Somalia, as businessmen use them as the quickest way of getting around.

Staying in touch

The public telecommunications system in Somalia was almost completely destroyed after the outbreak of the civil war in the early 1990s. Today, however, there is a thriving telecommunications industry run by private companies. The charges for international telephone calls are the lowest in Africa. This is partly because the different companies are competing for customers, but also because the businesses do not pay any taxes. There are around 100,000 main telephone lines and 641,000 mobile phones in use in Somalia.

TV and radio

Radio Mogadishu is operated by the Somali government, and there are also around ten private radio stations in the capital. Two private television stations in Somalia broadcast the Arabic news station Al-Jazeera and the USA's Cable News Network (CNN).

⬤ Hormuud – one of several successful private telecommunications companies in Somalia – has its headquarters in a modern building in Mogadishu.

DID YOU KNOW?

There are only three internet hosts in Somalia – the lowest in the world. There are 106,000 internet users in the country.

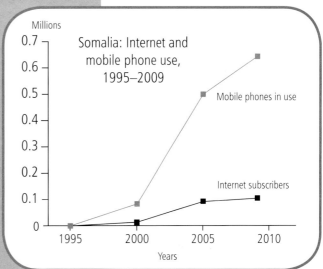

Somalia: Internet and mobile phone use, 1995–2009

Leisure and tourism

There is little leisure time for Somali nomads, but the men, women and children who live in permanent settlements, in towns and cities, enjoy spending their free time meeting with friends to chat, shop or play. Sports, crafts and music are all popular leisure activities in Somalia.

▼ Weaving is a traditional pastime in Somalia. People usually weave baskets for their own use, but sometimes they make them to sell.

Art and music

The Somalis are known for their crafts such as pottery, woodcarving and basket-making. These have long been part of nomadic traditions in the country, as nomads used the materials around them to make items that were both useful and beautiful. These crafts are still popular in Somalia.

Music in Somalia also draws on the people's tribal history. Ancient oral traditions of storytelling have evolved into music called *heello*, which is a type of poetry recited to music. Native Somali instruments include the oud, a stringed instrument a bit like a lute, and the batar drum.

Football fans

The Somalis are keen football fans, and young Somalis enjoy meeting friends for an informal game as well as watching professional football matches. There are several football clubs in Somalia, which take part in the annual Somalia Cup. The national football team is the Ocean Stars. Several Somali footballers have gone on to play for some of Europe's top teams.

Tourism

The Somali minister for tourism has been described as having 'the hardest job in the world'. There is no real tourism industry in the country – people are afraid to travel to Somalia because of the conflict there. However, if the situation becomes more stable, tourism could play an important part in the country's future. With its kilometres of sandy beaches and many sites of historical interest, there is much to attract visitors to Somalia.

⬤ Like young people all over the world, Somali children enjoying spending free time with friends. Here, they are at a local playground built from old vehicles.

DID YOU KNOW?

The Somali national anthem is called 'Somalia Wake Up'. The words of the song speak of a desire for unity and an end to violence.

Environment and wildlife

Somalia faces several environmental issues. The most serious of these are soil erosion and desertification, which make the land unsuitable for growing crops. Despite this, Somalia is still home to a wide variety of birds and animals that manage to survive in the dry climate.

Environmental issues

Because Somalia is so dry, water is a key issue in the country, and it has become even more serious because of the recent drought. There are not many natural freshwater sources, and only the Jubba River flows all year round. Most Somalis do not have access to clean drinking water. Overgrazing, drought, desertification and soil erosion have all badly affected the land, and this is destroying the livelihood of the nomadic peoples.

▼ Water pollution is a problem in Somalia, and contributes to the spread of disease, as many people use contaminated supplies for drinking water.

Natural resources

Somalia has many natural resources, including uranium and reserves of metals such as iron ore, tin and copper. It is likely that Somalia may also have some oil and natural gas reserves, and organizations including the World Bank believe that Somalia might one day be a major supplier of these resources. At the moment, though, the fighting in Somalia means these reserves are inaccessible.

Wildlife

The greatest variety of wildlife in Somalia is found around the Jubba River basin. Here, giraffes, buffaloes, hippopotamuses and camels roam, along with big cats such as lions, cheetahs and leopards.

There are several national parks in Somalia, but most of them are situated in areas that the government has no control over. Because of this, there is no one to stop the animals in the parks being hunted for food or trade, so their numbers are declining.

▶ The Somali, or reticulated, giraffe is native to Somalia, Ethiopia and Kenya, but very few are now found in the wild due to poaching.

DID YOU KNOW?
The leopard is the national symbol of Somalia. There are two leopards on the Somalia national emblem, standing on either side of a gold-bordered blue shield.

Glossary

ancestry people you are descended from, before your grandparents

autonomous having a certain amount of self-government

civil war war between people within a country

colonized when people from one country settle in another country and govern it

currency the money used in a particular country

democracy a form of government where people elect others to represent them

desertification the loss of habitable land into desert

drought a shortage of rainfall

erosion the wearing away of rock or soil by wind or water

ethnic belonging to a particular human group with common traditions and culture

exports goods or services that are sold to another country

extended family members of a family beyond mother, father and their children

famine a severe shortage of food

fertile land that is good for growing crops

freshwater inland water that is not salty

GDP the total annual value of goods and services produced by a country, measured over a year

Horn of Africa the easternmost part of the African continent

imports goods or services that are bought from another country

independence freedom from the control or influence of another country

infrastructure the basic services and equipment a community needs to function

literacy the ability to read and write

livestock animals that are raised to sell

malnourishment a condition where someone does not have enough food to function properly

mystical to do with sacred beliefs

nomads people who move around rather than settling in one place

oral traditions the spoken stories, from one generation to the next, of a people's cultural history and ancestry

overthrown when someone is removed from power without the process of an election

poaching killing animals when it is illegal to do so

ransom money paid to get something or someone back when they have been taken illegally

refineries places where impurities are removed from oil so it can be made into other products

remittances money sent back to a country by people from that country who live abroad

rural to do with the countryside or agriculture

scholarships money given to people to help pay for their education

tanneries places where animal skins are processed so they can be made into other products

textiles cloth or fabric that is usually woven

transitional government a temporary government intended to rule until a new permanent government can be established

tropical climate a climate in which there are high temperatures and high rainfall for most of the year

urban to do with towns and cities or life in towns and cities

Topic web

**Use this topic web to explore Somali themes
in different areas of your curriculum.**

Citizenship
From 1969 to 1991, Somalia was under the military leadership of General Mohamed Siad Barre. Find out what life was like for citizens of Somalia during this time. What changes did the military government introduce? How did these affect daily life for Somalis?

ICT
Use the internet to find a recipe for a typical Somali dish such as *muufo*. How is it cooked and eaten? Find out how to say 'hello' and 'goodbye' in Somali.

History
Somalia became an independent country in 1960. Before that it was colonized by Britain and Italy. Find out how these countries came to rule Somalia. Which parts were ruled by which country? How do Somalis celebrate independence day each year?

Geography
Find out the names of the five biggest cities in Somalia, and how many people live in each. Look them up on a map.

Somalia

Maths
Work out approximately how many times the UK would fit into Somalia.

Science
There is a small mineral industry in Somalia, which produces minerals including feldspar, gypsum, quartz and limestone. Find out about each of these minerals. What are they used for?

Design and Technology
People have lived in Somalia since prehistoric times, and ancient cave paintings have been found in parts of the country. Find a picture of these paintings on the internet and then draw one of your own.

English
Imagine you live in the Somali capital, Mogadishu. Using the information in this book, write a short story about what life is like. What might you learn at school? What do you do in your free time? What sights and sounds would you see and hear when you were out and about?

Further information and index

Further reading

Somalia (Moving to Britain) by Cath Senker (Franklin Watts 2008)
Somalia (Major Muslim Nations) by Joseph Ferry (Mason Crest 2009)
Somalia (Cultures of the World) by Susan M. Hassig (Marshall Cavendish 2007)

Web

www.bbc.co.uk/news/world-africa-14094503
The BBC news page for Somalia, with recent events and background information.
www.cia.gov/library/publications/the-world-factbook/geos/so.html
Information and statistics on Somalia, including geography, people and government.
www.unicef.org/somalia
UNICEF's Somalia web page, with news and features on the crisis in Somalia and what the organization is doing to help.

Index